A Convergence Of Tributaries

Notes from a Wayfarer

Courtney Glenn

BookLeaf
Publishing

India | USA | UK

Made with ❤ on the BookLeaf Publishing Platform

www.bookleafpub.in

www.bookleafpub.com

Dedication

For Matthew, Laney, and Julia, without whom my heart would know no rhyme.

Preface

A Convergence of Tributaries is a lyrical exploration of transformation, resilience, and the cyclical nature of creation. Anchored by the recurring image of the **coracle** – a small, ancient vessel symbolizing vulnerability and endurance – this collection navigates the shifting tides of memory, love, and identity.

From intimate reflections on relationships and loss to mythic meditations on time, ritual, and the cosmos, these poems traverse inner and outer landscapes, uncovering relics of meaning throughout the journey. Whether drifting down streams of self-doubt, mapping celestial patterns, or surrendering to the vastness of the wild unknown, *A Convergence of Tributaries* revels in the beauty of impermanence and the courage inherent to charting one's course through the murk and the light.

Acknowledgements

To my parents – thank you for weathering the storms of my youth with such unwavering patience. You provided a safe harbor for me when the waters were rough, and gave me the strong moorings I needed to launch my own ship with confidence.

To Matthew – my guiding light, my North Star – thank you for helping me chart a course through the unknown and illuminating the way with your unyielding love. You are my compass, my steadfast sail, and the anchor that keeps me steady in a world gone adrift.

And to all who sail alongside me, thank you for sharing these waters.

A Coracle at the Delta, Part I

A tenuously tethered thought,
tenderly lashed by the turbid waters of surreality,
strains effortlessly against the waxing of the wave.
Awash in the fertile moonglow of promise,
a shift occurs.
A silty slippage unfetters that notion
by way of cavernous contemplation,
and downstream it drifts,
seeding every ripple with purpose.

The Soothsayer, Asleep

"The future doesn't see as well
as we like," I tell you.
And it's true;
the last time I invoked *forever*,
I learned I was no prophet at all.
So now, I claim blindness
to the palm-lines of my heart.

But I am not unseeing; I simply lack faith
in things written in stars,
transcribed on cards,
or spied through some fish-eyed crystal
that looks clear only to those
still choking on the hearts
in their throats.

So I'll not entertain predictions,
and I'll not make any of my own.
But fear not, my dear:
while I make no soothsayer's claim,
if I knew I'd die tomorrow,
then I could confidently say,
"I will love you for the rest of my life."

Ignition

A spark goes dancing down the fuse,
sprung from its birthing place of
friction and fate. It is the envy
of the listless, who marvel at how
it magnetizes so swiftly to its prescribed path;
to leap at the moment of inception
from origin to purpose is the dream
of every poor wanderer walled in by
the expectations imposed upon them
by the complacent.

Their unwitting captors paper their own walls
with platitudes for polite company,
and any fire they may conjure
from their compact tinderbox
is quickly contained in slow-burning stasis,
waiting to be snuffed.
To harness fire for comfort is ingenious indeed,
a testament to the resilience of wild souls
who yearn for the safety of domestication.

But every once in a while,
it's best to unceremoniously smash
the chert against the quartz

and let the spark go dancing,
with anticipatory grace,
all the way to the oblivion
of creation.

Heron Reflection

The heron paused when I paused,
her beak poised for attack
over the great, mirrored expanse
beneath her.

Walking, I'd spotted her slender neck
as she, too, walked – her reedy legs
bending with slow, awkward grace,
and I watched as she picked her target
with a sly marble eye piercing
the gloss of reflected light.

But the heron stopped when I stopped;
and her jeweled prey shimmered,
retreating
into a dark algae embrace,
safe at last from that glass-cutting beak.

And I,
who only wished to observe,
who only meant to spare her the sound
of heavy steps on peaty ground,
watched the mirror ripple instead
as her silvered wings spread,

her bird's patience
expired.

Orbit

If I were a planet, and you a star,
what would our celestial pattern be?
I could circle you, adhering to our
knowledge of heliocentricity.
Or you might choose to orbit me instead,
as the churchmen of old insist you do.
Or we'll forgo what Galileo said
and ignore those ancient clergymen too,
marking a path unknown to anyone
in astronomy or theology:
where sometimes my earth will orbit your sun,
and sometimes, you'll revolve around me.

First Frost

Before the winter comes the frost,
the world is dull beneath its gloss.
A frozen blanket, gleaming gray,
turns night into synthetic day
as ice reflects the moonlight glow.
But frost must soon relent to snow,
and gray will yield to falling white
pure in day, natural in night.

A More Temperate Clime

I once knew love as a ten-minute rain
beating against the cracked clay
of a never-ending Texas August.
I rejoiced with every drop released
by that brooding cloud —
but they were too few, and only
made my parched landscape sizzle
with each thirsty, unmet need.

And once, love came hot as a breath
against a February windowpane:
a heated rush that fogged the glass
in a blurry circle. There, I traced
a fingertip heart, and there, I watched
its simple shape fade as cool clarity returned.

It was April that brought promise
with its more temperate clime.
Now, I keep my window open
to breathe in the scent of fertile earth
and the tiny blooms that have taken root there.

The Fire Circle

I am the ritual, I am the trance,
I am the fire around which we dance.
I am the spirit that moves from within,
I am the ending from which we begin.

I am the drummer, I am the drum,
I am the arm and the hand and the thumb.
I am the water, I am the fish,
I am the wisher, I am the wish.

I am the tether, the fettered, the free,
I am the sum of the two -- I am three.
I am the mountain, I am the cave,
I am the fear in the hearts of the brave.

I am the fire around which we dance,
I am the ritual, I am the trance.

The Necromancy of Silence

I am the keeper of words unsaid
and every thought suppressed;
I walk these earthen catacombs
without the hope of rest.
I cannot pause to light my way
or tie an errant lace,
for there's an ancient secret
to this godforsaken place:
the words and thoughts entombed within
this cold, unhallowed ground
all lie in wait to reanimate
and pull their jailer down.

The Harpstring Sings

This pearl of silver
poured from Myth into Being
within these bone-barred walls –
I lately hear it whistling
as it spins so fiercely
the eye cannot detect its movement.
We see it only with our opened hearts,
and they must withstand the sting
of being laid so bare
in such a sand-blown world as this.

But, oh!
The rapture our hearts will feel
as at long last, our lifeblood
flows with the iridescence
of Wisdom,
and the whispered strands of silver
mend that necessary wound
with harpstrings that will play
forevermore, so that our souls
can dance our Being into Myth
and back again.

A Coracle at the Delta, Part II

Where tributaries converge,
an idea must prove itself balanced,
buoyant, and watertight.
Tranquil reverie is best suited
for meandering streams;
rivers test the arrogance of dreams,
leaving wood-ribbed carcasses
of would-be river-tamers
along its ever-eroding shores.
Water cannot be domesticated
by the slapping of oars
or the churning of motors,
but a clever craft — a coracle, perhaps,
that taut, upended drum of a vessel —
is well equipped to ride the rush
from conception to birth,
for it is as cyclical and dizzying
as life itself.

The Fisherman and the Relic Hunter

The old fisherman, coarsely cocooned
against the cold, is at last
fully roused by the curlew's elegy.
He listens to the mournful song,
his mind hazily crafting lyrics lamenting
what was lost in yesterday's flood.
By lamplight, he had tried to count the casualties –
old netting needles, a dented mug –
but midnight mist had swallowed the remains
of everything left untouched (or only lightly jostled).
Now, in startled remembrance,
his aging joints give way to boyish fluidity
and spring him from the safety of his hearth
into the stubbornly stationary brume beyond.

Returning to his boat, he surveys the wreckage
as dawn wrestles with the fog.
His eyes sweep from helm to stern,
and then they ache with absence.
His father's oar, whittled by the waves
that once ferried his family
from blight to bounty, was gone –
slipped from its housing, slapped by waters

suddenly roused into rebellion.

The fisherman shakes the age
from his stooped frame and trudges
through the muck to his brother's boathouse
just a stone's throw down the shore.
The shed was boarded up near a decade past;
the old relic hunter had drowned on dry land,
gripping his bedposts as consumption
gripped his lungs. The fisherman
has not visited since, but now he must
weather the sting of his brother's death anew,
so their father's modest legacy might live.

Heralded by the crash of dilapidated planks,
the victorious sun chases the shadows
back into the waiting arms of dust and mold.
The fisherman's eyes flicker about, as unsettled
as the motes swirling erratically in the blinding beam.
Shelves stacked with a pitiful plunder
of silt-caked curios of wood and tin
creak and clatter with every cautious step.
Peculiar pursuits had always driven
the relic hunter, and forty-six years of
dredging the shallows for Roman trinkets,
Celtic idols, and Viking spearheads
had consigned his children

to an inheritance of algae and rust.

The fisherman could almost forgive
this impractical style of living –
before they knew famine,
they were adventuresome boys –
but he simply couldn't abide
the curious choice of craft his brother
constructed for his eccentric trade.
A coracle in lieu of a punt or a pram,
all hide and sinew and warped willow bands?
He may as well have hunted treasure in a soup tureen!
The fisherman laughs, imagining
his late brother, the crouton:
bobbing down the bog in a bowl,
parting the bulrushes with a ladle
and scooping seasoning from the sediment.
And now I must become the crouton,
he muses, his heart strangely buoyant
as he pulls the paddle from its peg
and yanks the coracle from its crypt.
Almost weightless in its simplicity,
the fisherman carries the craft
with near as much ease as he once
carted his drunk and lanky nephew home,
while his brother looted bog bodies
by lamplight.

At the shore, the old fisherman kneels
and readies the vexing vessel
for its spinster's voyage. Settled inside,
he traces the twine threaded through
the supple but watertight hide,
his callused fingers caressing
the carefully curated adornments
lovingly sewn into the brim
of – could it be? – this invaluable chalice.
With a ceremonial shove of the paddle
into the peaty lip of the tributary,
the fisherman launches himself
with twirling anticipation,
a born-again relic hunter
in his explorer's ship,
prepared to excavate his legacy
from the silt of obscurity.

Departing a City at Night

There is a certain sincerity
to the way people pause and look
through the portholes of a plane
when departing a city at night.

A near-hush settles,
perhaps a scattered sigh or two,
when travelers feel the urge to gasp,
but turn their breath swiftly
into quiet exhalations. Nothing more.
Maybe they're just tired.

Still, sincerity lingers
in the crowded cabin air,
as darkness and distance chase away
all the grim reminders of humanity below:
the harsh geometry of streets
and the arrhythmic din of traffic
ever on the edge of gridlock.

From such a vast vantage,
momentarily free of the strictures
of earth-bound existence,

the lights below become colored stars,
imploring us all to rediscover night.

Thermal Runaway

I thought to myself,
He is a supernova,
and intended
right then and there
to write a poem for you,
but our daughters – tiny tyrants –
obstructed my noble pursuit.
I return to the idea
one day later,
and it occurs to me
that I know nothing of
the ins and outs
of supernovae.

A quick search tells me
there are two types:
the thermal runaway and
the collapse of an elderly star.
I know you best
as a hot-footed runner,
and so I choose the former.
I learn that two white dwarves
sometimes become entangled
in their binary system, and so

they undergo
a reignition of nuclear fusion
so fierce, that they unbind into
pure energy and scattered star stuff
in a blinding flash.

The point, I think, is this:
in a star system bent
on your undoing,
you have learned
to burn brighter
than any light
imaginable.

The Garden of Delight

What might one do with a seer's sight
if not espy this garden of delight?
To see the satyr and nymph together
bounding, traipsing, free of tether,
drinking nectar of divinity
offered freely from the tree
that feeds all creatures high and low:
the sacred root from which we grow.

To know this place, to see it full,
the light of Earth, by right, must dull.
And we may find ourselves lamenting
a darkness that feels unrelenting.
We wander through this muted plane
seeking Heaven's light in vain,
and often, when we find a spark,
in our hunger, we snuff it dark.

It happens, though, upon a time,
we find a flame that glows sublime
upon this shrouded, shadowed sphere
that isn't fully there or here,
but rather serves as bridge between
the worlds of seen and of unseen.

I have found this light in you,
my muse, my faith, my purpose true
And through this flame I know my way
From earthen night to Heaven day.

Scraps

I know you didn't mean to leave
these pieces lying round –
you couldn't have anticipated
how heartbreakingly profound
it is to spy the little scraps
of paper shifting in the air,
disturbed by slowly pacing feet
(a single, solitary pair).

For Cordelia

Cast early from the laurel on the eve of spring,
your lips are petals silvered by the frost.
I hold this feather here, I see it trembling;
you live, my love, though breath and voice are lost.

The Coyote Steps Into the Spiraling Yonder

This cannibalistic dance of creation
is all we ever know.
The sex and the slaughter of limitless wonder —
simply look, if you will, to the spiraling yonder,
and see:

A surgeon's hand, steadied,
scalpel and forceps readied
to rend, with orchestral precision,
these cacophonic visions
from a lidless third eye,
and — delicately — assemble humanity
on cave walls and stone tablets,
on papyrus and sheepskin,
on the pulp of things that grew from seeds,
which now seed our dreams
with the music of whatever any of this means.

Caught in the swell, we people the well,
and carve rosettes on the bones
of the creatures that feed our wild, wild hunger.
And we send them, too, into that spiraling yonder —
over our cookfire, we feather the flames,

and signal the smoke to reach for higher ground,
where the gods look down
and nod.

"Yes. Yes!
Yes, this is what we have made,
and it is good."

So good, that even the coyote,
the pauper of beasts,
will someday spiral his way into a king
and feast.

A Ritual Transcended

A bath was once a sacred thing to me:
a warmth in the chill of an empty temple,
an alcove — cozy, but no less holy —
in which I sought sanctuary
from the vast and echoing halls of my loneliness.

I made secret offerings to you in the water,
which took from me my whispered prayers
with all the gentleness of a kindly old priest,
come to lead me out of the darkest night of my soul.

I had lived so long ensconced in skepticism,
that I had grown tired of my own agnosticism.
The bath seemed the most innocuous place
to explore my newfound religion.

Once submerged, this dearth of faith
was quickly replaced
by the most zealous of belief.
I was high priestess in a week,
and this bath was my holy throne —
but to the larger world I was a heretic,
and so I kept my worship silent, without fanfare.
I wore no robes.

Like all good heretics, though,
I longed to be united with the object of my reverence.
A bath only keeps its heat for so long,
and martyrdom is extremely warm.
Just ask Jean d'Arc.

And, like all good heretics,
I broke the fetters of pomp and ritual;
even the humble altar of my tub was suddenly too
profane,
for holy unions are made through spirit and flesh.

It has been almost three thousand days
since I was raptured.
I am now one with you, the creator
of all things good.
I am immortal in the heaven of our love,
and I have transcended the need for shrines
in my beatitude.

The Soothsayer, Awakened

Wordless in wonder,
I look out to the astral fields
that Time has turned for me.

When last I walked these rows,
there was not enough fruit
for a full harvest, and the meager yield
was bitter besides. Even the starlings
with their scavengers' tongues
left them to shrivel, or perhaps
for fodder to fatten their worms –
a more nutritious offering.

Doubt made for inhospitable soil,
save for my once-favorite crop,
irreverence. Barbed and squat,
it grew in a staggered formation
of spined sentinels baiting the brave
to pluck the prickled prize
that promised only diminishing returns.

Time has plowed this parched plantation,
his archaic machine inefficiently
fueled by every small victory deferred,

each cruel and unforgiving word,
either spoken or inferred.
Stooped with these burdens shifted
from my own weary back to his,
he has made a dance of his labor,
further complicating his path
for an audience that cannot
comprehend its aesthetic.

But, oh – to see these ethereal furrows
now, from where I stand at the rise
of the ridge, stargazing down upon
the bounty grown from tirelessly tilled
skepticism and scorn –
I am reborn.

Wings sprout from leaves of grass
and propel me with a purpose renewed
by faith, which was once so foreign to me.
Dreamlike, I drift through the vineyards,
wheatfields, groves, paddies, and orchards
all bursting with fruits, each one exotic
and wondrous to its neighboring crop.
As I come upon Time, still hunched at the handles
of his rusted rig, I join in his strange jig.
"How," I plead, "have you sown satiety
from the fissured soil of my youth?"

And Time, inglorious ploughman,
who so rarely pauses in his path,
turns to me with an infinite grin,
and conjures a seedling, straight out
of the electric air between us.
I palm the precious sapling
and bring it to my face,
but I don't have to look at it to know.
I feel the thrum of fertility.

In my hand, I hold Hope,
the origin point of all creation:
that coveted seed that was planted in me
the moment you answered my call.

A Coracle at the Delta, Part III

Ceaselessly spinning,
the coracle drifts and dances
between the reedy shores of unrelenting flow.
With slavering momentum
fed solely by its own perpetual potential,
the thought that was adrift and without form
now adroitly maneuvers its circular self
straight into the brackish swirl.
Spilling from the mouth of the delta,
the coracle cuts through
the briny spume of inception,
and, at last, unburdens itself
by surrendering to the vastness
of the wine-dark world
of reality beyond reason.